INNOVATORS IMPROVING TRANSPORTATION

Robyn Hardyman

LUCENT
PRESS

Published in 2020 by
Lucent Press, an Imprint of Greenhaven Publishing, LLC
353 3rd Avenue
Suite 255
New York, NY 10010

Produced for Lucent by Calcium
Designers: Paul Myerscough and Simon Borrough
Picture researcher: Rachel Blount
Editors: Sarah Eason and Jennifer Sanderson

Picture credits: Cover: Shutterstock: andrey_l; Inside: Copyright @ Ablinq Media: p. 27; BYD | Build Your Dreams®: p. 45; Carla Cargo Engineering: pp. 30, 31; Elio: pp. 3, 7; Photo courtesy of Eviation Aircraft: p. 38; Ford: p. 12; H2Fly/Jean-Marie Urlacher: pp. 1cl, 39; Luminar Technologies: p. 33; Jason Lutz Photography: pp. 8, 9; Nuro: p. 32; Oxbotica: pp. 36l, 36r, 37; Photo courtesy of Proterra: p. 10; Riversimple Movement Ltd: p. 21; Shutterstock: Chesky: pp. 35, 44; Rob Crandall: p. 19; Hazartaha: p. 4; Koptyaev Igor: p. 17; IVASHstudio: p. 26; Jarretera: p. 13; Matej Kastelic: p. 40; LightField Studios: p. 43; Metamorworks: p. 25; OlegD: p. 23; Rhonda Roth: p. 18; S-F: pp. 1l, 5; Stockcreations: p. 16; Tupungato: p. 24; VDB Photos: pp. 1r, 22; © Solar Impulse / Jean Revillard / Rezo.ch: p. 41; Sono Motors: pp. 14, 15; Thor Trucks: p. 11; Ujet: p. 28; Velometro: p. 29; Wikimedia Commons: Gnangarra: pp. 1cr, 34; Tim Strater: p. 6; Zunum Aero: p. 42.

Cataloging-in-Publication Data

Names: Hardyman, Robyn.
Title: Innovators improving transportation / Robyn Hardyman.
Description: New York : Lucent Press, 2020. | Series: Earth's innovators | Includes glossary and index.
Identifiers: ISBN 9781534565517 (pbk.) | ISBN 9781534565524 (library bound) | ISBN 9781534565531 (ebook)
Subjects: LCSH: Transportation engineering--Juvenile literature. | Transportation--Juvenile literature. | Motor vehicles--Juvenile literature.
Classification: LCC TA1149.H37 2020 | DDC 629.04--dc23

Printed in the United States of America

CPSIA compliance information: Batch #BS19KL:
For further information, contact Greenhaven Publishing, LLC, New York, New York, at 1-844-317-7404.

Please visit our website, www.greenhavenpublishing.com.
For a free color catalog of all our high-quality books, call toll free 1-844-317-7404 or fax 1-844-317-7405.

Contents

Chapter 1 Improving Today's Systems 4

Chapter 2 Electric Vehicles 10

Chapter 3 New Fuels 16

Chapter 4 Tackling Congestion 22

Chapter 5 Driverless Vehicles 32

Chapter 6 Aviation 38

Innovators of the Future 44

Glossary 46

For More Information 47

Index 48

IMPROVING TODAY'S SYSTEMS

The world is a very busy place. There are more than 7 billion of us living here, and at any one time, billions of people are on the move. We travel to and from school and work, and we go on vacation. We transport goods around the world by air, sea, and road. All this puts our transportation networks under huge pressure. Around the world, countries face the same challenges in improving transportation, and people are working hard to come up with innovative solutions to those challenges.

Too Many Vehicles

Transportation today faces two main challenges. The first is overcrowding. Anyone who has ever tried to drive through a city during rush hour knows this. In the United States alone there are about 260 million cars. The city of Los Angeles,

Our cities are choked with cars and other vehicles that create pollution. This pollution causes serious damage to the planet.

Some cities, such as Amsterdam in the Netherlands, encourage cyclists by making special bike lanes for them.

California, is adding cars at a rate four times faster than it did in the 1990s. The number of vehicle-miles traveled keeps on increasing, too, even though one-third of all trips are just 2 miles (3.2 km) or less. That is not sustainable because our roads and cities cannot cope with this volume of traffic. Our planet cannot cope either. This is the second challenge.

Damaging the Planet

Transportation is the largest and the fastest-growing source of greenhouse gas emissions in the United States. Greenhouse gases are released from vehicles that run on gasoline and diesel, as well as by factories. They collect in Earth's atmosphere and trap heat. This is making the world heat up in ways that damage the environment. This problem is the same around the world. We need to find ways to reduce the damage that transportation is doing to the planet.

Start Small

There are many innovative ways to tackle this challenge. Some are on a large scale, like redesigning our city transportation networks, or finding new fuels to power our vehicles. Others are on a very small scale, such as individuals choosing to take fewer car rides. Perhaps we can walk those short distances instead, or ride our bikes. Rachel Benyola thought so. She lives in Philadelphia and wanted to encourage people to ride bikes, so she designed a helmet that cyclists would want to wear because it looked great and was not bulky. She invented The London, a helmet made up of black triangular sections. It not only looks great, but it also folds up so that it can be packed away. It is a small innovation, but every step helps.

Step by Step

When you go on a journey, you have to start from where you are. It is the same with tackling the challenges of transportation. The problem is urgent, so we must start now with solutions that improve the systems we already have. Step by step, we will progress on the journey to make our systems less congested and kinder to the environment.

Better Design

We have to accept that people love their cars and that, in modern life, we need them to keep our economy going and to connect people.

So innovators are looking at ways to reduce the harmful effects cars have on the environment. The energy company Shell has worked with the engine specialist Geo Technology and an auto designer, Gordon Murray, to come up with a new concept car. This is an ultra-efficient city vehicle that, compared with a typical city car, uses 34 percent less energy over its lifetime. It produces fewer emissions than normal cars, weighs 1,212 pounds (550 kg), and is made from materials that can be recycled. Although the car will not be manufactured for sale, it has been made to show what collaboration between

At the Shell Eco Marathon, the most energy-efficient cars compete to travel the farthest using the least energy.

The three-wheeled Elio is attracting a lot of attention across the United States.

experts can achieve. The lessons learned will be very useful for future car design.

Efficient Fuels

Another area of innovation is making the fuels in cars work harder to deliver more miles for fewer gallons. Shell holds a competition every year called the Eco Marathon. This invites students to design their own ultra-energy-efficient vehicles. Thousands of young engineers form teams to design and build their own vehicles. They bring them to a track to test them and to see which one can travel the farthest using the least energy.

INGENIOUS INNOVATIONS

One U.S. innovator has come up with a more radical idea for a new vehicle. This is the Elio, a three-wheeled vehicle that looks a bit like a cross between a car and a motorcycle. Paul Elio designed it to meet the need for a small, efficient vehicle for city driving. His mission, as he says, was "To provide a fun-to-drive, super-economical personal transportation alternative, that's affordable, safe, and environmentally friendly." The Elio achieves an impressive 84 miles per gallon (36 km/l) of fuel, which is around twice as efficient as a standard car.

Supermileage

Engineers are looking to develop vehicles that can travel farther on less fuel. That makes driving both cheaper and kinder to the environment. One group of students, made up of Gary Ellingson, Caroline Sorensen, Eric Wardell, and Jared Lutz, decided to take on the challenge.

The best innovations in fuel economy at the moment are achieving up to 85 miles per gallon (36 km/l). This group, on the other hand, wanted to push fuel economy to the limit.

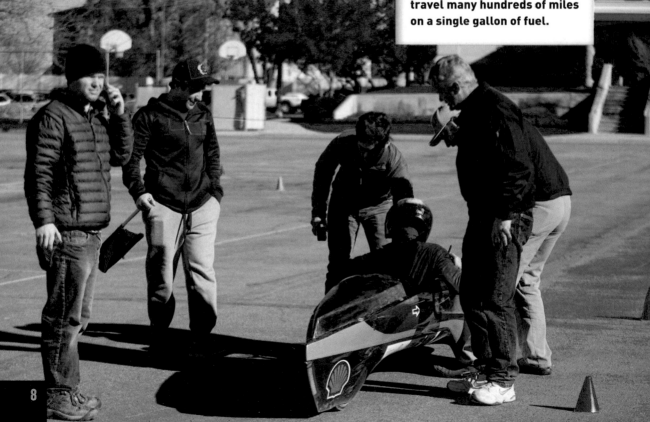

Ellingson and his colleagues set out to build a car that could travel many hundreds of miles on a single gallon of fuel.

The students' car is low to the ground, and has room for the driver only.

Teamwork

At Brigham Young University in Utah, Ellingson and his colleagues decided to design a car that could achieve more than 1,000 miles per gallon (425 km/l) of fuel. They hoped to take it to the Shell Eco Marathon (see page 7). The amazing car they came up with looks like a mini rocket, and it certainly can travel a long way on one tank of fuel. In fact, this supermileage vehicle achieved more than 1,300 miles per gallon (553 km/l). They drove it from Utah to Michigan on a single tank of gas.

Light and Sleek

The vehicle is very light in weight at 99 pounds (45 kg). In fact, the driver needs to weigh more than 130 pounds (59 kg) to give it enough weight for the road. The design is very streamlined to make it cut smoothly through the air. It also has a modular construction, so that the parts can be easily removed if they need to be repaired or replaced. It sits low to the ground, but has glass panels so the driver can see all around.

Slow and Steady

Can there be any disadvantages to this super mini-rocket? Although it looks like a rocket, it cannot exactly achieve rocket-like speeds. In fact, its top speed is around 25 miles per hour (40 km/h). That is how it manages to travel so far on so little fuel. Also, the driving position is almost lying down, and there is only room for one person—so it could be a lonely ride. We may not be seeing this car out on the road anytime soon, but the inspiration, ingenuity, and innovation this team brought to its project have shown what can be achieved.

CHAPTER 2

ELECTRIC VEHICLES

One of the biggest areas of innovation in the drive to reduce the harmful emissions that our transportation is currently producing is electric vehicles. Already some cars are hybrid, which means they run on electricity as well as having a conventional fuel engine. The car decides which power source to use according to the conditions it is in. There are some vehicles that run entirely on electricity, but there are some challenges with this technology that experts are working on.

Powerful Batteries

An electric car has to store that electricity somewhere. The storage comes in the form of a battery. The battery is charged using cables plugged into the main electricity supply. The technology challenge is to make a battery that can store enough electricity to power the car for a reasonable number of miles. Drivers do not want to have to stop to recharge their car battery every 50 miles (80 km) or so, especially as it takes hours to recharge the battery.

Electric buses like this one from Proterra are a clean way to transport people around and between cities.

Thor Trucks run on electric batteries, and release no harmful emissions into the atmosphere. Two members of the Thor team, Dakota Semier (left) and Giordano Sordoni (right), are pictured here.

However, storage capacity of car batteries is improving all the time. Innovators, such as the electric carmaker Tesla, have successfully developed batteries that can drive for around 300 miles (480 km) before needing to be recharged.

Clean Buses

In the fight against air pollution, cities around the world are also looking to use more electric buses for public transportation. Buses can hold much bigger batteries than cars, so they can travel farther between charges. One innovative company in California, called Proterra, broke the world record in late 2017 when the electric bus it has developed traveled for 1,102 miles (1,773 km) on a single charge while on a test run in Indiana.

Clean Trucks

It is not only passenger vehicles that are going electric. Trucks are following this trend, too. One company helping to make this happen is Thor Trucks in Los Angeles. Thor Trucks researches and builds battery-powered electric vehicles for commercial use, such as fleets of trucks for delivery businesses. The diesel-powered trucks that thunder along the freeways create a lot of harmful emissions, so this is an important contribution.

Charge Points

Of course, electric vehicles need places to recharge. More and more cities are putting in charge points, on sidewalks and in parking lots. Japan is leading the way and now has more electric car charge points than gas stations.

Renewable Electricity

Some innovators are going one step farther in their search for vehicles that are even more energy efficient. What if there was no need to plug the vehicle into the electricity grid because it could power itself? These are cars that run on sunshine.

Powerful Sun

Solar power uses the energy in sunlight to create electricity. This is done using solar panels in a process called photovoltaics, or PV. The panels are made using thin wafers of a material called silicon. The panels absorb the energy in sunlight and turn it into an electric current. The electricity that is created is then stored in a battery. Innovators are working on cars, airplanes, and boats that are powered by solar energy.

The car-manufacturing giant Ford has produced a trial car with solar panels on the roof. As it drives around in the sunshine, it is making its own electricity from the panels. It produces enough electricity to run the car for about four hours. This idea is still in development, but it is a glimpse of the way forward. Solar-powered boats, however, are on the water already.

Ford's C-Max Solar car has solar panels built into its roof, so it can generate electricity while it is outside.

Sun on the Water

Race for Water is a French organization dedicated to promoting the use of renewable energy. It has built a large boat that is covered in solar panels to help power it. The Yacht Club of Monaco in Europe has created an event to encourage innovators in solar-powered motorboats. Every year, these creative engineers come together to race their boats around the seas off the coast of Monaco.

INGENIOUS INNOVATIONS

It is not just the sun that is being used to power transportation. In the Netherlands, trains run on electricity. That is nothing new because electric trains have been around for decades. However, these trains are unlike others because they are all powered by the wind. In 2017, the Dutch government decided to stop using electricity generated by fossil fuels, such as coal and natural gas, to power its trains. Instead, the electricity comes from wind farms, where giant turbines convert the energy of the wind into electricity. This inspiring innovation is transporting close to 1 million passengers a day, with no emissions at all.

All the trains in the Netherlands run on electricity generated through wind power.

Sono Motors

In 2012, Jona Christians and Laurin Hahn had an important conversation about oil. These two young German engineers were concerned about the damage that oil and its products, such as gasoline and diesel, were doing to our transportation systems and our environment. They set about building a model in Jona's garage, to prove to the world that a solar-powered car could be made to help gasoline-powered cars become a thing of the past.

On the day their model drove up and down the driveway, they were truly excited. The two friends set up a company in Germany, called Sono Motors, to take their idea to the next level. They went online to raise funds for their project, and found that people were really interested in it. With the money they raised, they put together a team of engineers, electricians, designers, and business advisers to try to make their idea a reality and to get their car on the road. They call the car the Sion.

The Sion is built using lightweight materials so it is easier to power. Its battery can be charged like a regular electric car, as well as by its solar panels.

The team at Sono Motors, including Christians (left), Hahn (right), and Navina Persteiner (center), traveled through Europe in the Sion. Along the way, they asked people that they met for feedback about the car.

Start Small, Think Big

In July 2017, they finally presented the Sion to the world. The response was really positive. For three months, a team of six people drove the Sion all through Europe, showing it off and constantly checking the car's performance on the road. The tour went so well that they did the same again in 2018. More than 8,500 people in more than 30 countries have ordered one of these amazing cars.

How does it work? The Sion has solar panels built into its bodywork on the roof, hood, and sides. These convert the sunlight into electricity and store it in the car's battery, under the hood.

When the battery is fully charged, it can run the car for about 155 miles (250 km). But it can also charge as it runs, if there is enough sunlight. In the right conditions, the solar cells generate enough electricity to cover about 18 miles (30 km) per day. That is perfect for a car for city life. People can even use the Sion's battery to charge other devices, such as a laptop or cell phone. This truly innovative car looks set to become the future of city driving.

CHAPTER 3

NEW FUELS

There is no doubt that our use of gasoline and diesel is harming the planet. Billions of vehicles are emitting greenhouse gases that are contributing to the gradual warming of our world. In the United States, for example, Houston, Texas, has the highest level per person of greenhouse gas emissions, and transportation is responsible for 48 percent of those emissions. Fortunately, innovators are looking at an important way to address this problem, and that is finding new, cleaner fuels.

Big Innovators

Developing new fuels is an expensive business. It is mostly the big players who can afford to invest in this kind of innovation. The energy giant Shell, for example, is spending billions of dollars to support innovation in biofuels. These are fuels made from living things, particularly plants, so they are renewable. They can be mixed with gasoline and diesel to make these fuels cleaner, too. Most biofuels today are produced from corn or sugarcane. In Brazil, Shell works with Raizen, a local company, to produce biofuel from sugarcane. This fuel has 70 percent lower emissions than gasoline. In Thailand, Shell works with producers of palm oil to make biodiesel.

These pellets are made of wood chippings, a waste product from timber production. They can be burned as a biofuel.

Huge tankers like this one deliver LNG to ships across the oceans of the world.

Trucks and Ships

Ships and trucks run mainly on diesel and fuel oil, and these are high polluters. Innovators are looking at replacing these with a different kind of fuel: liquid natural gas (LNG). This produces lower levels of emissions, even though it is a fossil fuel. How can this gas run a truck? The answer is that the gas is cooled to -260 degrees Fahrenheit (-162 degrees C), which turns it into a liquid. It can then be stored in a tank, just like gasoline. Engines that use LNG are quieter, too, which is an added benefit in our noisy city streets. Shell is developing a network of LNG fuel stations for heavy-duty trucks in the United States, starting in Texas, Louisiana, and California. It is also working with China, where more than 200,000 trucks and buses use LNG.

LNG has the potential to be used by ferries, cruise ships, tug boats, and barges, too. It is already in use in Norway as a fuel for vessels on inland waterways. Huge vessels loaded with LNG will sail the oceans to refuel vessels as they need it.

17

Hydrogen

There is one fuel source that has many people excited. This is hydrogen, which is one of the most abundantly available substances on the planet. Hydrogen is a gas at room temperature and it contains a lot of energy. It is that energy that scientists think has huge potential for transportation because using it to power vehicles does not produce harmful emissions.

How Does It Work?

Unlike with standard fuels, hydrogen is not burned in a car's engine. It is used in a fuel cell inside the vehicle to generate electricity, which is then used to power an electric motor that drives the car. Inside the fuel cell, hydrogen is combined with oxygen and, in the process, it makes water and electricity. This is very clean energy because the only waste product is water, and that is so clean that you could drink it. So the fuel cell is a bit like a battery that can never die, as long as there is a supply of hydrogen in the tank. This makes hydrogen cars more attractive than standard electric cars with a limited range. Drivers can also fill the tank in a couple of minutes, instead of waiting hours for a battery recharge.

Currently there are a number of small-scale projects around the world using hydrogen fuel cells for transportation. Aberdeen in Scotland, for example, is running the world's largest demonstration project of hydrogen fuel cells. It has 10 public buses that are driven around the city.

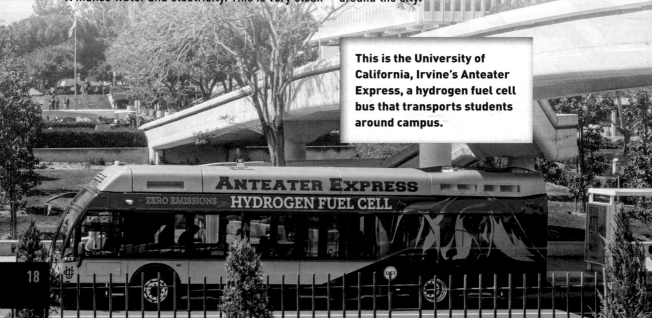

This is the University of California, Irvine's Anteater Express, a hydrogen fuel cell bus that transports students around campus.

Downsides

There are some disadvantages to this technology, however. Although hydrogen is abundant, most of it is locked up in water. Extracting it from water uses machines that are powered by electricity. Even if that electricity comes from renewable sources, it is not a very efficient way to make the hydrogen-based energy. The amount of energy you get from a hydrogen fuel cell is also less than from gasoline and from a standard electric car with a battery. You need to use more hydrogen to travel the same distance. Some experts think we should be concentrating instead on making better batteries that can take electric cars farther on a single charge.

INGENIOUS INNOVATIONS

No new fuel technology is going to take off if there are not enough refueling stations available. In Korea, one innovative company, Hylium, has produced the world's first mobile hydrogen refueling station. A huge truck carries enough liquid hydrogen to refuel 100 cars a day.

Hydrogen fuel pumps are beginning to appear alongside regular pumps at some gas stations.

19

Riversimple

Hugo Spowers is a British engineer on a mission. He wants to see major changes in the technology that powers our cars, so that we can make our transportation more sustainable. Spowers is not waiting for the big businesses to invest their millions of dollars in this, however. He is doing it himself. Spowers has designed the Rasa—a sleek car powered by hydrogen fuel cells.

Spowers studied engineering at Oxford University, in the U.K., and began his career in the motorsport industry, designing and building race cars. Seeing the impact that these cars were having on the environment, however, he left the industry and decided to develop his own, "clean" car of the future. He set up a business in Wales, U.K., called Riversimple, and got to work.

The Rasa

The Rasa is the first Riversimple car on the road in the U.K. It is a hydrogen-powered car that with a full tank can be driven for 300 miles (482 km). That is a very efficient use of the fuel. It is possible because the car is lighter, as it has no heavy engine or battery. The best electric cars can do about the same mileage on a single charge, but recharging takes several hours. Refueling a hydrogen car takes a couple of minutes. A trial of 20 of these innovative vehicles is putting them to the test.

What makes the Rasa different is that, unlike most new cars in development, Riversimple has not simply taken out the engine and replaced it with hydrogen fuel cells. Instead, it has scrapped all existing car designs and started fresh.

Hugo Spowers believes his innovative car, the Rasa, can make an important contribution to changing the way we drive and own cars, so that we stop polluting our planet.

Spowers's car has a motor on each wheel, for example. Every detail of this sleek two-seater is designed to make the car perform better.

No Ownership

Anyone who owns a car knows that it is expensive to run, and over time, it loses its value. After a few years, you need to replace it. Spowers has changed all that, too. You cannot own a Rasa.

Instead, you pay a monthly fee to drive it. That amount includes the fuel and all the running costs of the car. When you no longer want to drive it, you simply give it back. This means that Riversimple needs its cars to last as long as possible, to pass on to new customers, so they build them to do that. Spowers has had a lot of interest in the Rasa, and hopes it will be available for drivers in 2020.

CHAPTER 4

TACKLING CONGESTION

There is no avoiding the fact that our roads are congested. With more than half of the world's population living in cities, our streets are filling up with more and more cars, trucks, and buses. This is a problem for the environment because of the pollution the vehicles cause, but it is also a challenge for society. If people cannot get to work and goods cannot be delivered on time, it damages the economy and makes people stressed. All the experts agree that this is a major problem that we need to solve, but how?

Changing Behavior

Many solutions have been suggested. Should we charge people money, or tolls, to drive into cities or use the freeway? This is not popular with people, and politicians do not want to introduce charges that will stop people from voting for them. The best solutions change people's behavior, rather than punishing them for continuing in their old ways. There are many innovative ideas for making changes to how cities work, so that walking and biking are the easiest

Innovations, such as public bicycles for rent, are encouraging people in cities to leave their cars at home.

ways to move around, and public transportation runs quickly and efficiently. These changes make people choose to leave their cars at home. Some cities reward drivers financially for avoiding peak hours. Others design safe cycle lanes on the most popular routes, or pleasantly green routes for people to walk to work.

In the United States, for example, New York City has half the national average of greenhouse gas emissions. The city has taken innovative steps to achieve this. For example, it mapped the locations of where children were having asthma attacks, and found most were at major roads and interstates. This data helps people understand the impact of traffic on health. Once they understand, they are more likely to make healthier transportation choices.

Around the World

In developing countries, the problem of congestion is just as serious. The streets may be full of cars, buses, bikes, trucks, and animals, in an uncoordinated jam. There is little public transportation. The roads are often poor quality and there are few means of directing the traffic. Accidents are very common. Solving the problems of congestion will help these countries develop their economies, by making the transportation networks run smoothly.

Traffic congestion and pollution is just as bad, if not worse, in developing countries where many vehicles and people compete in crowded streets.

Car Sharing

Most cars are in use only 5 percent of the time. For the other 95 percent of the time, they simply sit in a driveway, garage, or parking lot. The idea that we each own our own car and use it in this way may soon belong in the past. There are many innovative ideas about how we can have access to cars when we want them, without this wasteful and inefficient system.

On Demand

Transportation on demand is an important area of innovation. Millions of passengers wanting a ride already use apps on their phones to call Uber or Lyft, two of the biggest companies providing taxi services this way. One recent report says that more people now use these ride-sharing services than take buses.

Other businesses take the idea a step further, using car-sharing services to reduce the number of vehicles on the road. Zipcar is the largest car-sharing company in the world. It was cofounded by U.S. entrepreneur Robin Chase. She has received many awards for her innovative approach to improving transportation. People sign up for a membership to Zipcar, and then have on-demand access to a Zipcar, which is parked on the street or in a garage, in cities all around the world. They can rent the vehicle by the hour or by the day. The company estimates that every Zipcar takes 13 personally owned vehicles off the road. What's more, every Zipcar has its own designated parking spot, so drivers do not have to circle the block looking for one. That helps with congestion, too.

Zipcar is the largest of many car-sharing businesses. Drivers can pick up this Zipcar and rent it by the hour or the day.

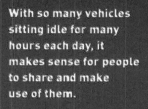

With so many vehicles sitting idle for many hours each day, it makes sense for people to share and make use of them.

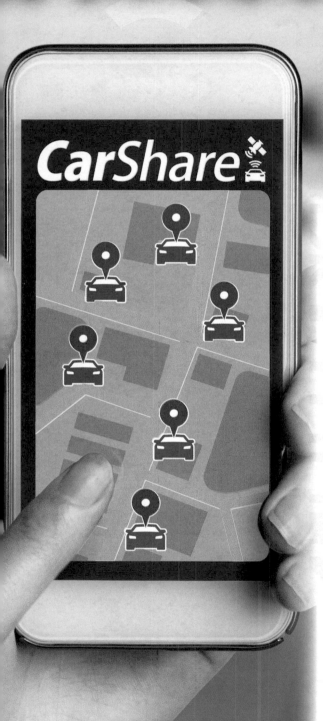

Putting Idle Cars to Use

Getaround, based in Los Angeles, is also for car sharing, but it uses people's own vehicles. Car owners put their idle cars to work by sharing them with people in their neighborhood, who can pick up the cars when the owner decides to rent them out. The owners earn useful money from doing this, and drivers get a car without having to own one themselves.

Rural Areas

Valerie Lefler of Nebraska realized that people in rural areas need help, too, especially because public transportation there is often limited. She set up Liberty Mobility Now, which connects local drivers with people needing a ride. It even coordinates with local public transportation, such as bus services. This new idea got off the ground quickly and is operating in seven U.S. states.

Smart Vehicles

Waiting in line at a bus stop can be time-consuming. The bus company runs its buses to a schedule, and passengers just have to wait for the next one. When the bus comes, it runs on a route that may not suit us, but the route is the same for every journey.

What if it did not have to be this way? What if the bus operators knew when people were waiting, and could send a bus along for them right away? What if they could also know where passengers wanted to go, and change the bus's journey to take the quickest route?

Innovators are working on the technology to make this happen, so that operators do not send out buses that nobody wants, and passengers do not have to waste their time waiting. This is called a smart system.

Book Your Bus

Bridj is an on-demand bus service. It uses real-time data on the traffic flow to plan journeys. Passengers use an app on their phones to tell Bridj when and where they want to travel, and Bridj uses all this information to deliver a pop-up bus service. The bus then stops at locations,

On-demand bus services save people time waiting at bus stops, and prevent buses from making unnecessary journeys.

which the passengers on board choose. If public transportation can be this responsive to their needs, people are much more likely to use it and to leave their cars at home. Bridj is still being trialed in Sydney, Australia, but this innovative idea makes great sense.

Get There Direct

Zeelo is a new company offering a similar service in the U.K., but it is designed to take people to events, such as sports games or business conferences. With thousands of people wanting to get to the same place at the same time, Zeelo coordinates their locations and creates a route to pick them up locally and take them there directly. People avoid lining up in their cars and searching for a parking spot, and it takes many private cars off the roads.

INGENIOUS INNOVATIONS

When a car accident happens, not only is it bad for the people involved, but it also causes traffic chaos. Hari Srinivasan of San Francisco, California, has created a phone app called Signal to try to keep accidents from happening. The app alerts drivers to safety hazards as they drive, such as dangerous intersections, pedestrian crossings, construction zones, potholes, bikers, and more. The system can build in information about changing weather conditions, such as ice, to its warnings about existing hazards. Signal also works with cities to improve their road signs.

Zeelo gets several passengers to an event at the same time. It means parking is less of a problem and there is also less congestion around venues.

City Streets

The streets of our cities are often noisy, smelly, and overcrowded. Too many people are trying to get somewhere all at once, especially in peak hours. The innovators of today are coming up with some truly inventive ways to get more cars off our roads.

The Ujet electric scooter is stylish, fun, and clean.

High-Tech and Stylish

Riding a bicycle is great, but it may not be a practical alternative if your journey is quite a long one. Cycling through busy city streets can also be quite a scary experience. One European company in Luxembourg, called Ujet, has come up with a new product to make traveling around the city safe and fun. This is an electric scooter that you can fold up when you reach your destination and carry inside with you. The battery, which fits inside the seat, can be removed and charged at any standard electrical outlet, and the scooter also has an onboard computer to give information about the area the driver is in. This is one high-tech and stylish solution to urban mobility.

VeloMetro in Canada has created another new way of getting around the city. This is the Veemo. The innovators at VeloMetro wanted to find a sustainable, affordable method of personal transportation that combined the best features of a bicycle and a car.

Like the Ujet, the Veemo is safer than a bicycle and more comfortable. It is an enclosed electric trike, so it protects the driver from the weather. The first fleet of these original vehicles is being tested in Vancouver.

Where to Park?

The problem of parking causes an enormous amount of congestion in cities, as cars circle the block looking for a spot. However, cities usually have plenty of private parking lots in great locations that are vacant a lot of the time, such as at offices and hotels and private plots of land. One innovative company called ParkBee has developed a smart technology that opens up these spaces to the public. Jian Jiang and Tom Buchmann in the Netherlands started ParkBee in 2015. After a successful first year, it spread to London in the U.K. Using an app, you simply put in where and when you want to park, and ParkBee finds a space for you to book.

The Veemo, an enclosed electric trike, is being developed in Canada.

Carla Cargo

All over cities, vehicles are making deliveries. Large and small trucks fill the streets as they take goods to stores and offices, and when they pull up beside the sidewalk, they cause even more traffic congestion. Some innovators are looking at new ways to tackle this problem, especially to deliver those goods "the last mile," which causes the most congestion. One of these innovations is Carla Cargo.

Carla Cargo is a bicycle trailer with a difference. This one has an electric motor and is designed to match the standard sizes of boxes in which goods are delivered. The idea arose among a group of four friends in Freiburg, Germany. They designed the trailer to carry and deliver vegetables grown by a cooperative to local stores and other customers, but they soon realized that the idea had the potential to be put to many more uses.

The Carla Cargo electric bike trailer is perfect for making deliveries. It is strong yet compact, ideal for navigating around narrow city streets.

Just about anything can be loaded onto a Carla Cargo trailer, including a refrigerated unit like this one.

Carry that Load

Bicycles are perfect for inner cities because they can navigate the traffic easily and quickly, and they produce no harmful emissions. With a Carla Cargo trailer attached, a bicycle can deliver a heavy load of up to 330 pounds (150 kg) to the most hard-to-reach addresses without causing any congestion or pollution. The trailer's powerful electric engine and sturdy wheels allow it to take heavy loads. Two heavy-duty brakes on the wheels also make the ride a safe and pleasant experience. The load can be protected with a waterproof cover.

Delivery to the Door

What makes the Carla Cargo trailer even better is that it can be attached to any standard bicycle or even an electric bicycle. So anyone with a bicycle can become a delivery rider just like that. The trailer's usefulness does not stop there. If the delivery is to a pedestrian area, or somewhere else not suitable for bikes, you can simply disconnect the trailer from the bike, lock up the bike, and wheel the trailer with its load right to the door.

People are finding many more things to do with a Carla Cargo trailer. You could load a mobile kitchen onto one and ride it to a festival or sporting event to sell food. You could use it to round up the rental bikes around town and take them back to their base. The limit is only the rider's imagination.

CHAPTER 5

DRIVERLESS VEHICLES

The most dramatic development in transportation since automobiles were invented more than 130 years ago is the driverless vehicle. It seems amazing that we could get into a car, tell it our destination, and sit back while it takes us there without us touching a steering wheel or a brake. Yet that is what the latest science is making possible.

A Solution?

Can driverless vehicles help solve our transportation problems? Since most driverless cars being developed are also electric, they are kinder to the environment. But could our roads simply remain congested with cars, but ones that function without us? The hope is that an autonomous vehicle, meaning one that drives itself, will be much more efficient at reaching its destination. It will be smart, able to communicate with other cars, and

Innovations such as the self-driving Nuro are a great way to reduce the number of short car journeys.

figure out the best route to suit the current traffic conditions. Certainly the technology is very exciting.

Large and Small

There are several big players, such as Google, working in the area of driverless vehicles, but there are also small-scale innovators working on this technology. Two ex-Google engineers, for example, set up a company called Nuro to develop a self-driving vehicle to be used for transporting local goods in their Californian neighborhood. The store loads up the vehicle with bags of groceries, and off it goes to deliver to local people. No driver, no passengers. It navigates hazards in the roads, traffic signals, pedestrians, and cyclists.

Starting Young

Driverless cars need sophisticated sensors to read the world around them and to respond as necessary. One innovator set about developing the technology for these sensors at a young age. He is Austin Russell, founder of Luminar Technologies. His sensor uses lasers to understand the world outside the car. It sends out pulses of light that bounce off surrounding objects and return to the sensor, building up a picture. Russell started his company when he was just 16 years old and studying at the Beckman Laser Institute at the University of California, Irvine. So far, Russell's company has raised $36 million to fund its research, and it now employs more than 250 people. After five years, the company is ready to start manufacturing its system to sell to customers who are developing autonomous vehicles.

Austin Russell's company, Luminar, is leading the way in developing sensors for driverless cars.

Taking It Bigger

If we can create a driverless car for our everyday use, why can we not create driverless trucks for transporting goods, and driverless buses for transporting people? The answer is that we can!

buses at London's Heathrow Airport to Austin, Texas, where the transportation authority is trialing an autonomous minibus service for the downtown area.

Take the Bus

Driverless buses are a great solution for taking people into the center of cities. People park their car in a parking lot a few miles outside the city, then board a shuttle to take them into the center. An electric, driverless shuttle means cleaner air, less noise pollution, and safer city streets. Pilot projects are starting up all over the world, from the Intellibus in Western Australia and passenger

Driverless Trucks

The next big thing in autonomous vehicles could be really big—a truck. One of the problems with driving goods all across the country in huge trucks is that drivers become tired. There are regulations on how many hours they can drive without taking a rest. If the person on board is not actually driving, surely there is no limit to how long a self-driving truck can keep going?

This Intellibus in Perth, Australia, is an innovative solution for transporting people in an environmentally sustainable way.

Driverless trucks can save fuel, too, because they accelerate and brake more gently than a human driver, using less power. Driving in convoys, they can tell each other when to slow down or speed up, to use fuel most efficiently. They are more likely to avoid accidents, too, knowing when to stay in lane, change speed, and avoid collisions. The trucks have a radar sensor system that monitors the road up to 820 feet (250 m) ahead. It sends out radio waves, which bounce back off other vehicles and hazards. These trucks still have a person on board who can take over if there is a serious problem. This means that truck drivers will not all be out of a job. It will be some time before we see only these trucks on the road, but it seems it could be the way of the future.

Driving in convoy, these driverless trucks can drive efficiently and safely, using the least amount of fuel possible.

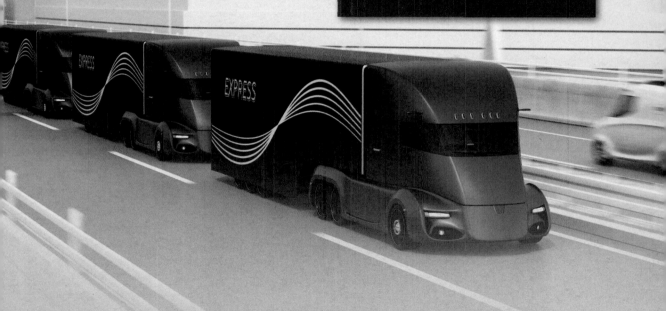

INGENIOUS INNOVATIONS

The vehicle manufacturer Daimler has created the Freightliner Inspiration Truck. It is the first autonomous truck to be approved for use on the road in the United States. It was cleared for use in Nevada and has been in action there.

Oxbotica

One of the world leaders in autonomous cars is the U.K. company Oxbotica. Two engineers at Oxford University, Paul Newman and Ingmar Posner, founded Oxbotica to challenge the tech giants of Silicon Valley in California. They are developing innovative software to make their autonomous cars the best they can be.

Newman and Posner built the U.K.'s first driverless car in 2012. Since then it has been a rocket ride. They are developing their new technology and exporting it around the world. Their technology is being used not just in cars, but also for transporting materials in mines, quarries, warehouses, and elsewhere. It is even being used beyond our world, on a rover vehicle on Mars.

Selenium

The software that Oxbotica is developing is called Selenium. Selenium uses cameras and lasers to tell the car exactly where it is, even in the dark. It then uses sensors and computers to spot and track every possible obstacle around it, from the curb and other vehicles to cyclists, pedestrians,

With their team, Posner (left) and Newman (right) have developed innovative software called Selenium to drive autonomous cars.

Oxbotica has been testing its driverless vehicle around city streets, and plans to test it on the main highway from Oxford to London in 2019.

and animals. Knowing where it is and what is around it, the system figures out a safe and efficient route to drive the car to its destination.

The Selenium software also learns from experience. So over time, its maps of the roads are updated with what it has seen, allowing it to become even better at finding its way efficiently. This memory can even share its information with other vehicles.

Fleets of Cars

Oxbotica has started taking its cars out onto the roads, and is convinced driverless cars are the way forward. The company has also developed a system for managing whole fleets of driverless cars. It is called Caesium. Caesium can schedule and coordinate the work of many autonomous cars at once, so that they can exchange data with each other as they go, to find the best and most efficient routes, all without a person getting involved.

As Professor Newman says, "We hope and expect that our technology will be adopted by vehicle manufacturers all over the world as the first wave of autonomous vehicles, as the public imagines them, comes to market."

CHAPTER 6

AVIATION

It is not just on our roads where we have transportation
challenges. We are taking more journeys by air than ever before.
Air travel contributes up to 10 percent of the greenhouse gas
emissions that are harmful to our planet because the powerful
engines that get planes off the ground burn a huge amount of
polluting fuel. Flying is essential for business, trade, and leisure.
We are not likely to cut down the number of flights we take in the
future, so we need to find ways to make air travel cleaner.

> Could we soon be
> seeing this Alice
> electric plane flying
> between our cities?

Electric Planes

Just as the automobile industry is working hard to bring more electric cars to our
highways, some experts in the aviation industry are developing electric planes.
It is noisy onboard a jet aircraft, but on an electric flight, your journey would be
silent! No more engine noise and no more polluting emissions either. One Israeli
physicist, Omer Bar-Yohay, is a pioneer in this field. He is the founder of a company
called Eviation. Eviation is developing a nine-passenger electric airplane, called
the Alice. It is designed for travelers who want to hop from one city to another on
relatively short journeys.

Designing an electric airplane means scrapping all previous aircraft designs, because standard aircraft are designed to carry heavy engines. An electric airplane has motors instead, which change electricity to movement. They can be placed almost anywhere, even on the wingtips or tail. The Alice can fly up to 650 miles (1,040 km) on a single charge of its battery, at a speed of about 275 miles per hour (443 km/h).

New Fuel

Battery technology is still not able to lift heavy airplanes to a high altitude and keep them flying there, but engineers think it soon will be, because advances are being made all the time. For now, attention is focused on smaller planes. The Hy4 is the world's first four-seater aircraft to be powered by hydrogen fuel cells. It was developed by a European team. It can fly for 10 hours with no emissions.

Hydrogen fuel cells power the Hy4 four-seater plane. The only waste product of this source of energy is water.

Fly Right

Some of the innovations in aviation are focused on making the planes more economical to run and more environmentally friendly. Others are looking at improving the experience of the customers, so that they want to fly again.

Flight Experience

Many innovations in aviation are behind-the-scenes improvements that make us more comfortable. The Crystal Cabin Awards is an annual competition to reward innovators who have come up with ideas for improving our journeys, from when we arrive at the airport to when we sit down in our seat. They include things such as how to fit more baggage in the overhead lockers, how to recycle the garbage passengers create onboard, phone apps for guiding the passenger through all the airport procedures, and ways to rearrange the seats on board to fit the maximum number of passengers in each class.

Long flights are tiring, so innovators are working on ways to improve the experience.

The amazing around-the-world flight of the Solar Impulse was the dream of just two people, but it has opened the way for innovations in aviation that promise to change the way we navigate the world.

INGENIOUS INNOVATIONS

If we can build solar-powered cars and boats, why not planes? One innovative organization, Solar Impulse, believes we can. The idea for Solar Impulse came from two men in Switzerland: Bertrand Piccard, a pilot, and Andre Borschberg, an engineer. They had a vision of creating a solar plane that could fly right around the world, day and night, without fuel. And they did it. They created an ultra-light plane that is powered only by the rays of the sun. Starting in Abu Dhabi, in the United Arab Emirates, the Solar Impulse took off on the first stage of its flight. It remained airborne for longer than any aircraft in history, more than five days and five nights. Over the total around-the-world trip it flew 24,855 miles (40,000 km) without a drop of fuel. This extraordinary journey was watched with wonder by the world. It promises a new era in aviation.

High Fliers

Another innovation is designed to cut the time it takes to fly long distances. In 2004, entrepreneur Richard Branson of Virgin Atlantic started work on Virgin Galactic, promising to offer commercial flights into space to people who could afford it. The technology behind these flights could change air travel. If planes can fly much higher, to the edge of space, they can reach higher speeds. Today it takes 21 hours to fly from London to Sydney, Australia. Branson believes it should be possible to do it in just two hours.

Zunum Aero

Zunum Aero is a pioneering company in the world of electric aircraft. Aero engineer Matt Knapp founded the company in Kirkland, Washington, in 2013. Knapp is passionate about bringing high-speed transportation to every community in ways that do not harm the planet.

Knapp and his team are so committed to their innovation, they are confident that, by 2022, they will be launching commercial flights for up to a dozen passengers at a time. What's more, their hybrid electric planes will be able to fly these passengers between 350 and 500 miles (560 and 800 km). That is an ambitious target but Zunum Aero has the backing of world-leading aviation firm Boeing. Boeing will offer its technical expertise. In 2018, Zunum signed up their first customer, a charter air service in California called JetSuite.

Zunum electric planes could soon be transporting passengers on short flights between cities.

Battery Power

Two large battery-powered fans drive Zunum's plane. Power from a generator supplements the batteries, but this is only for takeoff and climbing—it shuts down once the plane reaches its cruising height. Zunum hopes that by combining the new electric technology with standard power methods, it will be able to get its project off the ground more quickly. As the company learns how well the plane performs, it can then progress toward making an all-electric plane as the technology for batteries improves.

City to City

The main market for this amazing new plane is flights between cities that are 350 to 500 miles (560 to 800 km) apart. Business executives make thousands of these journeys every year to meet their suppliers and their customers face to face. These short flights are especially bad for the environment, because it is the takeoff and landing that create the most pollution. They are also relatively expensive for the airlines to operate because they use so much fuel. Without the costs of the fuel, these flights will become cheaper and attract more customers. They can also use small airports, closer to the city centers that are the travelers' destinations. That will save the travelers time, which is a precious resource in the day of a busy executive.

The entrepreneur Elon Musk, founder of the electric car company Tesla, believes that all transportation will one day be electric. Could it be that, over the next 10 or 20 years, we will be boarding a silent, electric plane to take us on vacation?

Business travel is responsible for many of the plane journeys that cause so much pollution. Converting those journeys to electric planes would be a great step forward.

43

INNOVATORS OF THE FUTURE

As long as we have global problems to solve, pioneering work will always continue. Today's cutting-edge transportation ideas may seem like they belong in science fiction, but they could well turn out to be the solutions of tomorrow. We must continue to develop our STEM (science, technology, engineering, and math) skills and to think creatively to drive the innovations of the future.

City Streets

Many ideas for the future focus on making our city transportation networks function better. One idea is for moving walkways through our cities, like the walkways in airports that take passengers to departure gates. These would be faster, though, at up to 12 to 15 miles per hour (19 to 24 km/h), to compete with public transportation, and take far more people at one time. Just step on, hold on, stand still, and off you go. Or you can start walking, to get to your destination even faster. Most cars do not reach more than 15 miles per hour (24 km/h) in our congested cities, so this would be a great option at peak times.

In the Air

There is not much more space on the ground for transportation networks, so some

Science fiction or the near future? These blue electric drones are delivering goods, while the yellow taxi drone takes passengers. Both are relieving the crowded roads below.

SkyRail is an electric train that would run along major highway and freeway routes, but directly above them.

innovators are taking to the skies. VRCO is a U.K. company with very ambitious plans. It is developing a luxury two-person aircraft that will also be able to drive on roads and land on water. The NeoXcraft is a flying car and is the idea of Mike Smith and Daniel Hayes.

Surely the highest-profile transportation project for our future is the Hyperloop. This ambitious system would carry people between cities at up to 700 miles per hour (1,130 km/h). Passenger pods would whizz through a network of special tubes, driven by the power of magnets. Hyperloop was originally the idea of Elon Musk. Realizing this was a massive project, he made the plans public and invited engineers around the world to contribute their ideas. The Nevada desert has seen some spectacular testing by Hyperloop One, the company overseeing the project, and the development of this most radical project is now spreading around the world.

Innovation Today

Our busy world needs ingenious innovation in transportation today, tomorrow, and into the future if we are to meet the challenges of keeping everyone on the move while, at the same time, protecting our planet. Fortunately, there is no shortage of people committed to this work. Business entrepreneurs, research scientists, and even governments are all searching for innovative solutions to keep the world's wheels in motion.

Glossary

asthma a condition that causes difficulty with breathing

atmosphere the air around Earth

autonomous acting independently, without a driver

battery a container in which energy is stored, then converted to electricity when needed

biofuels fuels from living things, such as sugarcane, which are renewable

charter flights arranged for a particular journey, not part of a regular schedule

clean not creating pollution

collaboration working together

commercial describes a product or service that is made to be sold to the public

concept car a car built to show off new technology and design, rather than to be sold

congested extremely crowded and blocked

convoys groups of vehicles traveling together

cooperative a business owned and run jointly by its members

data information

developing countries poorer countries that are trying to improve people's living conditions

diesel a liquid fuel, heavier than gasoline

drone a pilotless aircraft

economy a country's industry, trade, and finances

emissions the release of something into the environment, particularly of pollution

entrepreneur a person who has an idea and starts a new business to develop it

fossil fuels energy sources found in the ground, such as coal, oil, and natural gas

fuel economy a measure of the amount of fuel a vehicle uses to travel a set distance

generator a machine that changes movement into electricity

greenhouse gas a gas, such as carbon dioxide, that traps the heat of the sun in the atmosphere

grid the network that distributes electricity from power stations to consumers

hybrid using both electricity and a conventional engine powered by diesel or gasoline

hydrogen fuel cells devices that combine hydrogen and oxygen to create electricity

lasers intense beams of light

motor a machine that converts electrical energy into mechanical energy

photovoltaics (PV) the process of creating electricity from the light of the sun

radar a system that sends out radio waves, which bounce off surrounding objects and return

renewable sources that do not run out, such as light from the sun, wind, and plants

sensors devices that detect physical conditions, such as light or sound

software instructions for a computer

solar relating to the sun

sustainable able to continue at the current rate; or a resource that will not run out, such as wind

turbines wheels used to change the movement of the wind or water into electricity

For More Information

Books

Marquardt, Meg. *Hydrogen Fuel Cells*. Minneapolis, MN: Core Library, 2017.

Olson, Elsie. *Biofuel Energy*. Minneapolis, MN: Abdo Publishing, 2019.

Verstraete, Larry. *Innovations in Transportation*. New York, NY: Crabtree Publishing Company, 2017.

Zuchora-Walske, Christine. *Self-Driving Cars*. Minneapolis, MN: Checkerboard Library, 2018.

Websites

The Center for Climate and Energy Solutions has all the facts to improve your understanding of climate change and how transportation contributes to it at:
www.c2es.org/content/climate-basics-for-kids

Find out about hydrogen and how this element could help solve our transportation problems at:
www.eia.gov/kids/energy.php?page=hydrogen_home-basics

For more information about the progress of Hyperloop, check out:
www.hyperloop-one.com

Read more about the Sion and how Sono Motors is tackling the problem of transportation at:
www.sonomotors.com

Publisher's note to educators and parents:
Our editors have carefully reviewed these websites to ensure that they are suitable for students. Many websites change frequently, however, and we cannot guarantee that a site's future contents will continue to meet our high standards of quality and educational value. Be advised that students should be closely supervised whenever they access the Internet.

Index

airplanes 38–43, 45
apps 24–25, 26, 27, 29, 40
asthma 23
autonomous vehicles 32–37

biofuels 16
boats 13, 17
buses 10, 11, 17, 18, 25, 26–27, 34

cars
  accidents 27
  autonomous 32, 33, 36–37
  congestion caused by 22–23, 44
  electric 10–11, 12, 14–15, 18, 20–21
  energy efficient 6–9
  hydrogen 18–21
  leasing 21, 24–25
  parking 24, 27, 29
  sharing 24–25
  solar 12–15
congestion 4, 6, 22–31, 32
cycling 5, 22, 23, 28, 30–31

delivery vehicles 30–31, 33, 44
developing countries 23
diesel 5, 11, 14, 16, 17
drones 44

electric charging points 11
electric vehicles 10–15, 18–21, 28–31, 32, 34, 38–39, 41, 42–43, 45

flying cars 44–45
fossil fuels 13, 17
fuel economy 6–9, 35, 43

gasoline 5, 11, 14, 16, 17, 19
greenhouse gases 5, 16, 23, 38

hybrid vehicles 10, 42–43
hydrogen fuel 18–21, 39
Hyperloop 45

lasers 33, 36
liquid natural gas (LNG) 17

pollution 4, 11, 22, 23, 31, 34, 38, 43

radar 35

scooters 28
sensors 33, 35, 36–37
solar power 12–15, 41

taxi services 24, 44
Tesla 11, 43, 45
trains 13, 45
trikes 29
trucks 11, 17, 34–35

walkways, moving 44
wind power 13